Ever Since The Accident

Nick Lovell

Black Eyes Publishing UK

Ever Since The Accident
By Nick Lovell
© Nick Lovell, 2019

Published by Black Eyes Publishing UK, 2019
Brockworth, Gloucestershire, England
www.blackeyespublishinguk.co.uk

ISBN: 978-1-913195-05-2

Nick Lovell has asserted his moral right under the Copyright, Designs and Patents Act, 1988, to be identified as the author of this work.

All Rights reserved. No part of this publication may be reproduced, copied, stored in a retrieval system, or transmitted, in any form or by any means, without the prior written consent of the copyright holder, nor be otherwise circulated in any form of binding or cover other than that in which it is published and without a similar condition being imposed on the subsequent purchaser.

A CIP catalogue record for this title is available from the British Library.

Cover design: Jason Conway, cre8urbrand.
www.cre8urbrand.co.uk

This book is dedicated to everyone who has shown support for me over the past six years, everyone who has encouraged me, advised me, taught me and given me a platform to perform on in that time. There are some people who deserve special recognition though.

Firstly, Ash Dickinson and Eley Furell for giving me the inspiration and encouragement to write my first performance poems and enter the 2013 Swindon Slam. Thank you so much! You honestly changed my life!

Then Marcus Moore, Sara-Jane Arbury, Melanie Branton, Robert Garnham. Angie Belcher, Jemima Hughes, Mab Jones, Johnny Giles, Emma Pursehouse, Peter and Josephine Lay, Brenda Read-Brown, Ziggy Slug, Chloë Jacquet, Jason Conway, Amie-Lee Richardson, Joy France, Hannah Walden, Binks Bin McWobbla and everyone that has shown such love and kindness along the way.

The Swindon poetry crowd, Scott Cowley, James Osborn, Sue Hammond, James Neill, Jonathon Robert Muirhead, Sharon Hooper and all of you that have helped inspire such a vibrant poetry scene in Swindon!

Clive Oseman, my co-host at 'Oooh Beehive' and travelling companion across thousands of miles driven in the name of poetry. Thanks mate. We make a bloody good team!

To my sister Gail... for everything.

And finally, my long-suffering wife Michelle and the three perfect living poems that I had a hand in creating… Chris, James and Josh. Sorry for the artistic sulks and forced exposure to poetry and thank you, for everything!

Ever Since The Accident

Contents

9	All for Some Not Some for All
10	Thief of Hearts
11	Crimson Tears
12	Field Trip
13	Forgotten pleasures
14	Market Garden
16	Ever Since The Accident
19	Puncture Wounds
20	The Fog of Peace
22	Happy Accident
23	Human, writes
24	Divine Wind
25	Natural!
26	Outside
27	Masks of Men
28	Pandora's Net
30	Bounce Doubt
31	Tears of a Clown
32	The Jinx Effect…
34	The Madness of Poetry
35	The Trouble with Bullshit
36	Ugly Truth
38	Kiss N Tell
39	Schrodinger's Cat
40	Where Waves End
42	Winter Break
44	Towering Shame
45	Heart Beat
48	Walk with a Stranger

All for Some Not Some for All

A bullet for the baker, for the postman, for the trades,
and uniforms and hours wasted standing on parade.
A whiskey for the Minister, some claret for his friends;
discussing how the bloody war affects investment trends.

Propaganda for the masses, jingoism to the fore!
Prison for the traitors who dare speak against the war.
Longer hours for the workers, more profit for the boss,
they can't leave it, they must take it, so he'll never make a loss

A mansion for the arms dealer, with patio and pools,
paid for by Daddy Warbucks and governmental fools.
A bailout for the bankers, so their bonuses are paid,
you can get away with murder knowing how the game is played.

A bullet for the Billies, for the Peters, for the Daves,
for the fathers, brothers, mother's sons, now lying in their graves.
Promotion for the Minister, largesse for all his friends,
supplied by the shady Arm's Dealer, on whom their game depends.

Thief of Hearts

Her voice sold dreams of beauty.
While they were distracted
by the heavenly melody of
her mouth and skin,
she rifled souls and stole tears,
sometimes breaking hearts
in scenes of accidental vandalism.
She played out their fears
deft fingers delicately dancing across
the black and white keys
of their padlocked minds.

Crimson Tears

You shook and I fell,
unable to tell where reality ended
and we began, as the steel slipped in
and your arms cried scarlet tears.
The pain of years screaming
from the dried tracks plastered over
the cracks in your smile.
Fist clasped, pin prick gasp,
till big baby blues oozed
blurred words of love.
I held you while you bled,
while you fell apart,
kissing your damaged skin.
wishing I could kiss
your bruised and damaged heart.

Field Trip

We lie our love from ecstatic lips,
dancing scenes from wet dreams
on a carpet of a million filter tips
and empty ten bags. A riot of slags
writhing before our saucer eyes,
whistles trill to steaming skies
while another pill thrills.
Beats spill from mind to muscle
each lost in the bustling heat.
Chill out time with foot long rips
as we lie our love from ecstatic lips.

Forgotten pleasures

I dreamed I could fly, that my broken body soared.
World spread beneath, every last detail clear
to my eagle's eye, freedom roaring like wind
beating against my ears as I lost myself.
Tossing and turning, crossing the beaming blue sky,
slowly learning control, attitude, speed.
Swooping down, proximity to the ground
the greater part of the rush, then up, up;
the Sun my goal, impetus bleeding joyously off,
tangential trajectory carrying me further aloft.
Soft, gentle seconds, movement frozen,
free of gravity, spectacular stillness. My world,
that solar stare seemingly inches out of reach.
A whisper of breath tickling my ears,
rising to a whoosh, a roar, a screech,
drowning my screams of delight
as I embrace the plunge.
Body lunging forward, stiffening, eyes narrowed,
every inch of skin alive with the roughness of air.
Buffeting, soothing, cares stripped,
the reckless abandon of my dive becoming all,
until the harsh dawn of reality calls.
Walls close in, hemming, restricting,
gravity once again constricting my shattered self,
landing me, grounding me.
A shop soiled, broken winged model,
forever neglected on a dusty garage shelf.

Market Garden

"I don't think I'm going to make it.
Would you stay,
and hold my hand?
It wasn't meant to end this way,
I had always planned
to live to be a hundred,
raise a family, build a home.
Now those dreams, like me, lie ruined
and I don't want to die alone.

The lads and me
were all so keen
to come and do our bit.
Thought we'd all
return as heroes,
like anyone would give a shit.
But one by one
they've been gunned down,
none spared till now but me.
Their blood and guts,
dunging fields
from hell to eternity.

Are you still there, mate?
It's awfully dark.
I thought it was only noon.
I'm sorry to have kept you here
but I'll be going soon.
These guilty bullets burn inside
like a thousand angry bees,
I can hardly feel your hand now mate.
Stay a little longer, please?

It would have been
my birthday next week,
I'd have had a score
of years and life beneath my belt,
But then this fucking war,
took hold of me, it twisted things.

It brought me here to die.
It taught me how to follow fools
and never question why.

Thanks mate, for your company,
for staying by my side.
I never thought I'd be so scared,
I guess needs must conquer pride.
Tell them it happened instantly.
Don't tell them about the blood,
nor my rasping breaths through gritted teeth,
nor my shit mixed with the mud.
Don't tell them 'bout my mangled leg
or the terror in my eyes.
Don't tell the truth of how I died,
just pass on my goodbyes."

Thousands died in Arnhem,
blazing pit of twenty hells,
where the devil danced to the endless beat
of a million artillery shells.
There, I held a dying young man's hand,
till his final rattled gasp.
Felt his hand clutch mine, that one last time.
Felt him shudder as he passed.
Felt the anger, rage and sickness
tear apart my tattered mind.
Felt the helplessness and terror
at the touch of graveyard lime, and knew
his youthful face, now still,
would live with me through all my time.

Ever Since The Accident

It took just a second.
A twitch of a hand,
a tick of the clock,
a flick of the switch.
It was that quick.
Monday morning
weather fine.
One moment, the monotony
of the drive to work;
the next, life on the line.

The windscreen dissolves
into a galaxy of stars.
Thoughts of work,
and the day ahead
are blown out of my head
by a bang and a jerk.
My life turns
upside down; spins me
around and around.
Floor becomes roof
roof becomes ground.
Sight and sound stretch.
Time holds its breath
as death slides expectantly
into the passenger seat
and my heartbeat slows.

The tick
of the
clock.
The flick
of the
switch.
Each slow roll
accompanied by the
tolling of car horns.
Screeches of surprise
from frightened tyres.

I choke back my screams
I don't want to go faster.
What seemed important
one tick
of the
clock,
one flick
of the
switch ago
is gone for good.
This sudden disaster
rewiring my soul.
My only goal is to survive.
To get out of this alive.

My rolling roadblock
rocks to a stop
and my life hangs
by a seatbelt.
The fervent prayer
that there isn't a lorry,
it's driver unaware
of anything but
his tight schedule,
bearing down to
end my new life
before it begins.

Darkness, dirt.
One shard of sun
turns dust to diamonds
as Death winks, then leaves.
I breath again.
Time speeds up.
The eerie silence
of the violence shatters
as footsteps clatter closer.
I fight and struggle
with the beautiful seatbelt,
trying to escape its
smothering embrace.

A race to the light,
wriggling, snaking…
Trying to make room
to escape this wreckage
this wasted tomb.
Like a baby from the womb
I'm born again,
recreating the sacrament
of birth. I lie
bloodied and stained
on the cool earth before
standing. Walking
my first baby steps
along a new path.

The one I have walked
ever since the accident.

Puncture Wounds

Shards of memory litter the floor,
piercing my bare feet, leaving perfect red footprints
that trace my path through sanity, through life,
forever towards the exit, towards the door.
Towards freedom.

The Fog Of Peace

Have you walked the Terminator?
The line that separates day from night,
dark from light, wrong from right,
knowing you are the thin red line
that keeps them apart?
I think not!

It's not there when I look at you,
it's not written in your face, your walk.
There's no dark angel outlined in your shadow
as you pass by,
no real hate in your dismissive glance.

Does the smell of blood wake you in the night,
cloying and rich in your nose?
Do demons dance around the fires
that burn in your dreams again and again
until you beg for release?
For mercy for your sins?

And is she there when you sleep?
Oh no, not her.
She will never wake you from your repose,
from that safe fantasy, fuelled stupor you call dreaming.
Real dreams bite harder, deeper, with fury and rage.

She comes to see me every night,
she talks to me, asks me 'Why?'
Where was I when the lines became blurred,
which side was I standing?
And on whose orders?
I cannot answer, for in her world
I am dumb,
whilst in mine I just feel dumber.

Any port in a storm.
anything acting like an off switch,
a stop switch, a standby switch.
Standby switch?

Bloody necessity switch more like.
Any respite from her less than gentle attentions
is welcome in whatever form it takes.
Liquid, powder, pill, potion or lotion.
The act like magic charms to keep me safe
in the arms of Morpheus.

When you drink it's to have fun,
get laid, make friends and influence people.
Well it's all the same really isn't it?
Drugs, you can take them or leave them.
Don't mind a bit of Charlie or weed at a party,
but, "Its a recreational thing, you know what I mean?
A bit of a laugh"
You lucky bastard.

So walk on by and go home
to your comfortable apartment
in that low rise, high price,
'but hey, you can afford it so why not?' block,
they built last year.
I'm sure you have earned it.

I ask little for me and my kind,
just that someone, somewhere remembers,
we still fight our battles
forever lost in the fog of peace!

Happy Accident

I walk down familiar corridors,
past memories lurking in shadowed corners.
Locked doors stretch into the distance,
disappearing into gloomy pasts.
Slight sounds heard through thick dark wood,
muffled yet familiar, the tone of a voice,
the barking of a long dead pet.
The sigh of a long-lost lover
prickling at my neck, caressing my skin
with nostalgia until goose bumps
form a dot to dot of every love's face.
The soft, regular sound of my footfall,
deadened by the thick dust of dreams
covering the floor, coating the handles.
Stinging my eyes to tears as each particle
burns my throat. Blurred vision;
a hundred corridors,
a thousand doors spinning
until I catch a flying, flashing handle.
Too scared to stay, yet too scared to run
to flee this choking nightmare while I can,
the soft sounds drowned by my racking coughs.
I bully my way through, senses reeling,
blinking tears from my burning eyes.
Feeling my way into memories,
hearing your voice for the first time in years.

Human, writes

Your words rise unfettered,
higher than the executioner's sword.
Stone breaks scissors,
scissors cut flesh.
Heads roll and
scarlet words gush forth,
steaming at their birth.
Each lettered wisp
dancing in the cold air,
spreading, unstoppable!
Rising unfettered
above your innocent blood.

Divine Wind

Finding only destruction
when my smouldering hands
fell from my eyes,
you hid and I sought.
Blinking at a new sun.
Stillborn.
Innocence swept away
by the violence of the wind.
Ears screamed into silence,
taking my friends, my city,
my world, as it passed.
This blast of vengeful breath
from the west.
I alone in my class lived.
Scarred, forever tarred
by Pluto's tattoos.
Some visible to all,
others only seen
by a survivor's keen stare,
should our eyes meet
and I glimpse
my city's death
remembered there.

Natural!

You didn't notice me,
either of you.
I was hidden,
separated by a thousand miles
and four millimetres of glass.
Your eyes only shone for each other,
your ears deaf to all but his voice.
The totality of your existence
and independence reduced
to each other's company.
I sat transfixed, mesmerised,
basking in the joy glowing
from your faces,
radiating from the way
you moved as one.
Oblivious of all
save yourselves.
Hand in hand, step by step,
you passed by, love unashamed,
unafraid, determined,
and oh so true.
I sat unnoticed,
jealous of the pair of you,
yet still warmed
by the fire of your passion
and the freedom in your hearts.
The tenderness in the way
you kissed your partner's shoulder,
so innocent, so natural,
so normal, gave me hope
that, for the rest of my life
I would see rainbows.

Outside

Sorry may be the hardest word to say,
but loneliness is a heavier load to carry.
So, I tarry here at the edge of the light,
watching the endless ballet of the night
from the other side of the glass.
Foot tapping to the muffled music
as Harry and Charli walk away
cheek to cheek, soul to soul.
Oblivious to all save themselves
as they roll home,
this night their past,
their future, drunken fornication.
They pass, leaving nothing
save fading echoes
of a lovers' conversation
and my vague sense of jealousy
at his hand upon her arse.

Masks of Men

As ghosts we gather,
shadows on the edge of sight,
Death's young apprentices
soon to be released
into the silence of the night.
Quiet our deadly trade.
Craftsmen of killing, masters of stealth.
Sharp blades, soundless strikes
our methods,
continued survival our wealth.
Boyish banter whispered,
quelling never admitted fear, then,
we part, each to our targets.
Young boys' faces
wearing painted masks of men.

Pandora's Net

Internet, intervene, interweave.
Deny, apply, deceive.
Implore, inflame, impeach.
Preach, teach, reach, use,
revile, renounce, abuse.
Facebook, racebook, hatebook,
what a fucking statebook.
Brickbats, intellectual spats, racist attacks.
Selfish selfies, pictures of cats,
facts debated, castrated, negated.
Hashtag, eco bag, dirty slag, fag hag.
Sanctimonious, acrimonious.
Youtube, you lose, use lube.
Adverts, infoverts, docudramas, perverts.
Awkward silence, sexual violence,
Netflix, netflops, box sets, chick lit,
cheap dreams, quick thrills, sick kicks.
Digital manipulation, cognitive stagnation.
Hatred dissemination, data assimilation…
"Which 18th Century Baked Pudding were you?
Click here to allow us access to your friends list,
your phone book, medical records,
girlfriend's naughty pictures
and internet banking password to find out".
First person, first on scene,
first pictures, worst pictures.
Captive audience,
unverified, terrified, terrorism.
Live feed, 24/7, newsjacked, redacted,
selective news, opposing views,
conspiracy heaven.
Utopian, multicultural,
dystopian, disturbing,
dysfunctional.
Perturbing, perverting.
Instructional.
Desperately seeking Tinder and Grinder.
Pornhub, quick rub, sly tug.

Brazzers expects every girl to do her duty,
to gobble and be obscene.
PVC, BDSM, casual meets, dogging
and the occasional freak
seeking a good old-fashioned relationship.
Spin, spin, spin, win, win, win.
Hate, hate, hate, casino cashing in on your dreams.
"Gamble responsibly and when the fun stops…
Ah fuck it, what have you actually got left to lose anyway?"
Delude, collude, allude.
Accusation equals participation,
result? Uninformed condemnation.
Social justice juries' rule on trials
by Twitter.
Echo chamber, stranger danger.
Embittered bigots spitting
vile bile, while Pandora laughs
the last laugh;
her box ripped open.
Now who controls the past?

Bounce Doubt

I curled up, like a ball,
hoping to bounce,
stay whole, undamaged.
For the first second,
I thought it had worked,
then I hit hard.
Smashed, shattered, scattered,
broken beyond repair.
I curled up, like a ball,
in pain.

Tears of a Clown

I am in tears,
but please, don't offer hugs,
love or sympathy.
These are good tears.
Ones conjured
by kindness or memory.
Ones that leak out
when clouds paint the face
of a loved one in the sky.
When the path is steep,
yet a willing hand reaches out
to keep you going.
The tears that fall
when a snatch of song
transports you, Tardis like, back to scenes
when bodies were younger
and the sun always stayed high.
Every diamond drop,
a forgotten smile,
a kind word given
on a difficult mile.
A pint drunk, a band heard.
Each silver trail
that tracks down my tired skin,
a path back to lost friends,
past times, magical youth
and manic grins;
the good times had.
So yeah, I am in tears
but believe me,
I am not sad.

The Jinx Effect...

Dear Sir slash Madam slash Miss slash Ms,

I am writing to complain about either the veracity of your advertising campaigns or the quality of your range of underarm deodorant products.

Since your range of products was released over 25 years ago, I have purchased 17,526 cans of the various aromas you offer, based upon your advertising campaigns indicating that I merely need to apply one small spray of any of your wide range of products to my body, to precipitate a veritable storm of beautiful women filled with desire as a result of sensing the aromatic bouquets that you have created and I have purchased...

It is my sad duty to inform you that not one of the cans I have purchased over the past two and a half decades has functioned as advertised and has not resulted in so much as a smile from any females at all, let alone the beautiful women depicted in your advertising campaigns... Not a bloody sausage!

At first, I thought this lack of response from the opposite sex may have something to do with the amount applied. As a result, I have increased the amount I apply to see if this has any effect. I currently apply approximately one can, per day... Per armpit... and the only effects I have noticed so far have been a certain light headedness for an hour or so after completing my toilet...and a mildly painful rash!

After several more lonely years I also considered the application methods and remote locations shown in your adverts and have to report that having travelled to every beach currently reachable by car, rail, boat, plane, submarine and helicopter in the inhabited world... Not a single girl approached me, unless you count the female lifeguard who interrupted my experiment on Bondi Beach to advise me that my interpretation of the ninja like moves essayed by the male model whilst applying deodorant in one of your television adverts...were disturbing people.

I am also disappointed to note that the large wooden ark I have built in my back garden has yet to attract so much as one short dark and ugly munter, let alone streams of blonde goddesses coming for me two by two... Whilst it has gained me some attention... Being named Noah on the front page of my local paper was not quite the result your adverts had led me to expect.

Having noticed with interest your campaign intimating that your products are of assistance in locating hitherto undiscovered tribes of

Amazonian beauties with a propensity to remove their underclothes to signify their approval of my choice of sachet… I have spent what free time was available over the last seven years, what with building a bloody ark and searching for that sodding beach…trekking across the world's last wildernesses and as a result can advise you that, despite attracting millions of biting insects, flies, spiders, scorpions, snakes and one over amorous brown bear, your various products failed to attract one single woman or even married ones…

Therefore, it was with relief that I viewed the adverts announcing the release of your His n Hers range of fragrances. This advert clearly demonstrated that these two new additions to your range are suitable for use in the urban environment and thus I purchased a case of the His variety and applied two cans of said range to each armpit. Once I was able to stand again and leave the house, I set off through the town centre, anticipating a wave of vehicular carnage with swarms of female volleyball teams tearing themselves free from the apocalyptic wreckage of myriad team buses, all overwhelmed with desire…. For me… Sadly the only vehicular mishap to occur as a result of my use of your product was due to the dizziness following my over-application of the spray. In my disorientated state, I staggered into the road and was struck by a lorry,

Undeterred I applied my reserve can to my body whilst in the ambulance and can now happily report that at last, after 25 years, 17,526 cans of your product, thousands of miles of travel, hundreds of miles of trekking, countless insect, fly, spider, scorpion and snake bites… one ark, one bear mauling and one life threatening road traffic accident… there has finally been a result. One of the nurses on duty in the Intensive Care unit has asked me for a date, once my legs heal and I can walk again…

His name is DEREK…

Thank you very bloody much indeed!

The Madness of Poetry

It's a flow, a beat, a rhythm,
this gift we've been given.
It's the singing of the soul
and the breaking of the heart.
It's the gathering together.
The tiny little spark
that sets ablaze the thatch.
An illness with no recovery.
The itch you have to scratch.
A scab we'll always pick.
The striking of a match.
A light in darker places,
the revolution's base,
a comfort and a worry wart,
a most peculiar place.
It's the fire always burning
the passion in our lives.
The wheel that's always turning
bane of husbands and of wives.
It's the beating of our drum,
the job that's never done,
the stories that need telling,
the wave that keeps on swelling.
It's the riptide in our blood
the chewing of the cud.
It's blood and sweat and tears,
hopes and dreams and fears,
coffees, fags and beers,
a jury of your peers.
It's the ounce of hope to keep you sane
in the hardest, darkest patches,
a feeling like no other
no love ever truly matches.
It's the wicked storm now weathered
the blooming flower in the desert.
It's the riffs, the rhymes and stanzas;
words and lines that flow in me
the reason we were put here;
It's the madness that is poetry.

The Trouble with Bullshit

Chemtrails criss-cross clear skies
above a London police station.
Inside Banksy improves
the quality of the graffiti
in a prison cell,
contemplating his next work,
which will prove
Man never stepped on the moon.
Upstairs the arresting officer
pauses in his scribbled report,
wondering how two buildings
can collapse so neatly.
At home, his wife nurses
their sick child;
dying for want of vaccination.
Sacrificed on the altar
of her parents' tabloid beliefs.

Ugly Truth

I see you, scurrying through the shadows,
clinging to the crepuscular,
the absence of light
sparing your secret shame.
Keeping out of sight a habit
since their calls of "you're ugly,
YOU ARE UGLY".
Sure, they lied. You know that
everybody tells you.
But, barbed words pierce young hearts.
Long after the shafts
are snapped and drawn,
the tips remain, buried deep inside.
Rusted nibs twist harsh words
into scars, pain scores each stroke.
Screams burn your throat
like vomit, every time you choke
down the memory of their hate.
Silent slave to the power
of one long gone, cruel comment.
A single moment, so strong,
ends your chance to belong,
to get on and make friends.
Your mind reminds you,
playing endless echoes
of voices chanting flick knife lies
in playground rhymes.
Each repetition picking
at the weeping scars
that never get a chance to heal.
Blood now falls from blade-torn skin.
The pain of committing the unforgivable
sin of difference stored in scars
and tracks from too many stabs in the back.
You constantly fight to make amends.
A different you every day,
chameleon trends a way
to be OK, just for a while.

Yet you can't bribe the past,
can't pay off the pain, so your account
remains forever in arrears
to the memory banks.
That's why you turn off the lights.
We sit in squid ink blackness
listening in your dark,
holding your hand.
Trying to understand
why my comfort can't compete
with your lifetime's pain.
I whisper my wasted words
Again and again…
You're beautiful.
You are beautiful.
You ARE beautiful.

Kiss N Tell

The smart tart departs
heart fluttering
muttering a simple goodbye,
no 'sorries…see you laters…or whys.'
He starts to speak, to seek her promise
but she is gone, footsteps tripping
along a hotel corridor, towards her
'Kiss and tell' future.
This one worth it
at last.

Schrodinger's Cat

Does Schrodinger's cat chase possible rats?
Stalk 'maybe' mice through the laboratory?
Kill probable birds, leaving their bodies
outside the box as gifts?
Does she or he…
Cats always seem female to me…
ever bat a ball of thread
from the fabric of time?
Do her paws trot with soft patter
across dark matter as she squeezes
through black holes in pursuit
of questionable voles or potential moles?
When she confronts Pavlov's dogs
in a theoretical battle of hypothetical wills,
does the gentle tinkling
of the bell around her neck
reduce them, one by one
to dribbling wrecks?
If she pauses
before scratching their noses
is it for a relative period of time?
Does she join other experimental cats
in quantum choruses of dimensional yowling,
heard only by the ears that hear
trees falling in deserted forests?
If, indeed, they actually fall in the first place?
Has she ever clawed the trousers of time,
rubbed herself in Moebius figures of eight
around paradoxical pairs of ankles
unworried that they might or might not exist?
When she sleeps curled up,
does the waveform collapse
as she dreams of reality?

Where Waves End

I meet you
where waves end
where screams fade
beneath the surf.
Where sorry does not count
and a million
Facebook shares
don't save.
...
I meet you
where dreams die,
swept out with the tide.
In the space between
ignorance and sympathy,
where cold shoulders
shrug away empathy
and hard hearted
politicians lie.
...
I meet you
where bigotry fights
forever bleeding hearts.
Where political wrongs clash
with human rights.
Where media agendas
dilute the truth
with right wing lies.
Where promises deferred
down out desperate cries
...
I meet you
where futures fade,
and the sun sets forever,
Where the time
is always too late.
Where humanity fails
and bodies float,
face down
in black waters,

sailed only by the Reaper's
dark boat.

I meet you
where waves end,
where tears begin.

Winter Break

Voices echoed back and fore
across the shattered landscape,
across that stark scene,
dressed with barbed wire,
strewn with human wreckage
and garlanded with mile upon mile
of shattered trenches.
No snow here, just mud
spread thicker than chocolate on a cake.
Deep and stinking,
clinging to cloth
and skin and memory.
Yet still, as the guns fell silent
and gentle rain hissed
on the hot metal of their lethal barrels,
voices rang out.
Foe calling foe,
enemy calling enemy,
man calling man,
brother calling brother.
Language no barrier.
While they shared few words,
their mouths shared
the same shy smiles,
their faces the same sorrows,
the same scars carved
deep behind the eyes of all present
more fraternal
than any shared tongue.
Handshakes and hugs
as men who, minutes before,
had been dedicated
to each other's slaughter,
fumbled for understanding
when faced with their neighbour.
Playful charades
and cosmopolitan mimes abounded,
gesturing hands
and grunting grimaces

conjuring cigarettes,
tobacco, flasks of cognac,
wine and the inevitable football.
It never mattered
who won or lost that day.
Just that the game was played
and for one brief moment,
sanity restored.

Towering Shame

The machinery
is broken,
rusted from
the flood of tears
that came too late
to quench the flames.
Vandalised by
the neglect of those
who now seek
to avoid all blame.
Short circuited
by Government ministers'
refusal to show any shame
for the delays
to laws designed
to prevent
the kind of mistakes
that cause these disasters.

Heat Beat

The golden gloating sun beats down as my cheaply shod feet pound the desiccated dusty drab ground and a million questions asked in Parliament pass over my hunched head and shoulders while the burning eye of Helios concentrates superheated heavenly hatred upon the blistered back of my neck stating its hatred in tattoos of scarlet pus filled packages carried on my neck and shoulders for days before painfully bursting with biting relief.

My footsteps clatter back at me from the unending row of faceless places where the rich ones live lives of unimagined luxury with china plates and polished silver cutlery served by hired hands who send as much as possible to families in far off lands to save and spend and build better lives where one day they will be waited on by impoverished millionaires their riches gone in one of those shady internet affairs where everyone seems to lose forever.

The black chipped paint of the front door smiles sun driven reflections in greeting then slams shut against the stifling roar of the baking world. God turned the heating up out there and popped out for a while perhaps to get some shopping perhaps to cure or kill a sick child and no one knows when he will return. The air conditioning hums softly as it begins its duty of turning the suet pudding sticky air into churning blasts of sweetest breath.

Cooler now I relax and unwind with a drink and a film and some self-abuse. As the catholic priests from my youth beat me not sparing the rod until my flesh was bloody and weeping when I was under their tutelage so I beat myself until my rod is raw the painful, joyful guilt of release heating my face despite the manufactured coolness of this artificial refuge, my private hidden place.

Breathless panting slowly subsides and boredom fills the void left inside my heart and mind as Lucy does Jane does Sam does Debbie does Dallas and I wonder at what point did these princesses' palaces come crashing down around their hearts and souls and how many goals were moved or blocked before eating pussy and taking cock for a living seemed like a good idea.

I cannot trust my thoughts not to end up disgusting me so I mentally change channels hitting the DVD stop button so the screen goes fuzzy and a hissing fills my ears like a thousand snakes rearing to attack and me armed only with a remote control. I press gently upon the off button, my finger caressing its curiously malleable surface as once again I shut it all down.

Still partly undressed I pace through the rooms of this cool corner of my private hell carefully constructed from the wreckage of my past. I kick doors open just to break the choke hold silence that clings to these walls each room holding sleeping memories, now disturbed. Cool evenings of musk and magic sweating nights of slick skins and tenderness as hands crawled over and under and around each other private picture plays on the insides of my eyes until at last I have no choice but to turn and quickstep to the front door fastening my trousers as I go.

The sun greets me eagerly blinding my eyes and flash frying my barely cooled skin back to irritated perspiration in seconds. My heart beating faster as my tarred and feathered lungs strain finding more moisture than air in each slobbered breath. Pain flashes like inspiration through the steaming sauna of my overheated brain and I look back at the house, wondering whether to turn around again but my feet save me from my cowardice and I place my trust in their regular plodding and follow their lead.

My strides guide me down paths where trees hold shady parades in blessed copses woods and groves the sun still cooking the shit out of the ground in the small glades between. Even the grass grows warm and crickets hide in the shade of rotted bark too hot to chirp or fiddle too hot to think about attracting a mate while my mind bubbles and seethes in its obscenely hot basin yet never too hot to stop composing internal hatemails containing truths that only the closest of witnesses could know.

My cheap shoes bite and pinch at my toes and heels as I walk. After a time, weals form, then blisters which burst before I even know they are there bathing my feet in a mixture of blood pus and sweat. Each sharp pain drawing a curse from my sun-dried tomato shredded lips as I spit rose red petals into the dust without thinking a lingering trace of my presence long after the liquid has dried. A cigarette fails to sooth my parched throat but I smoke it anyway the dryness of the smoke a delightful counterpoint to the dank heat of the day.

Eventually my treacherous feet lead me to where we once played together. Fields where we once lay together and I sit against a tree tears still hot enough to burn as they cut down my sun-scarred cheeks. Eyes closed although the sun still pulses orange through shuttered lids, I lose myself in those times. The years in which I earned your trust when we danced with the stars and slept in each other's arms. When beauty was in the eye of both beholders time was young and we were charmed.

Memories run through heart and soul as comatose and timeless I sit body and mind years apart with heart lost somewhere in-between until I realise that the sun has sunk low. My wits slowly gather like a murmuration of starlings banding together for their long flight south and I wrestle my way to my feet joints muscles locked into place by prolonged immobility conspire fighting my desire to rise and go. The heat and my thoughts ageing me in the flutter of an eyelid. Luna smiles down as I retrace my thoughtless steps back towards the empty house so full of pasts still lost within the disaster… I call myself.

Walk with a Stranger

Walk this wreckage,
ignore the attention of
the hidden man who follows.

Blind eyes seek
long dead places.
Fleshless fingers clutch
for balance.
Feet sunk deep,
the rotting mulch
of hope
disturbed for
the first time in years.

Small, careful steps.
down tangled paths,
forgotten pasts,
rubbish and waste.
Hands sifting
shattered images.
discarded hearts.
Detail lost in drifts of dust
buried beneath trunks,
fallen family trees,
no ties to support
their unbalanced mass.

The hidden man touches,
beckons.
Leads the way.
One last walk.

Nick Lovell is a part time commentator, full time optimist, half-arsed anarchist and occasional poet. He started writing and performing in 2013 and since then has won several slams across the country and in 2018 took part in the National Poetry Slam finals at the Albert Hall. He also co-hosts 'Oooh Beehive' in Swindon. He looks at life sideways, then writes about it!

www.ingramcontent.com/pod-product-compliance
Lightning Source LLC
Chambersburg PA
CBHW071322080526
44587CB00018B/3325